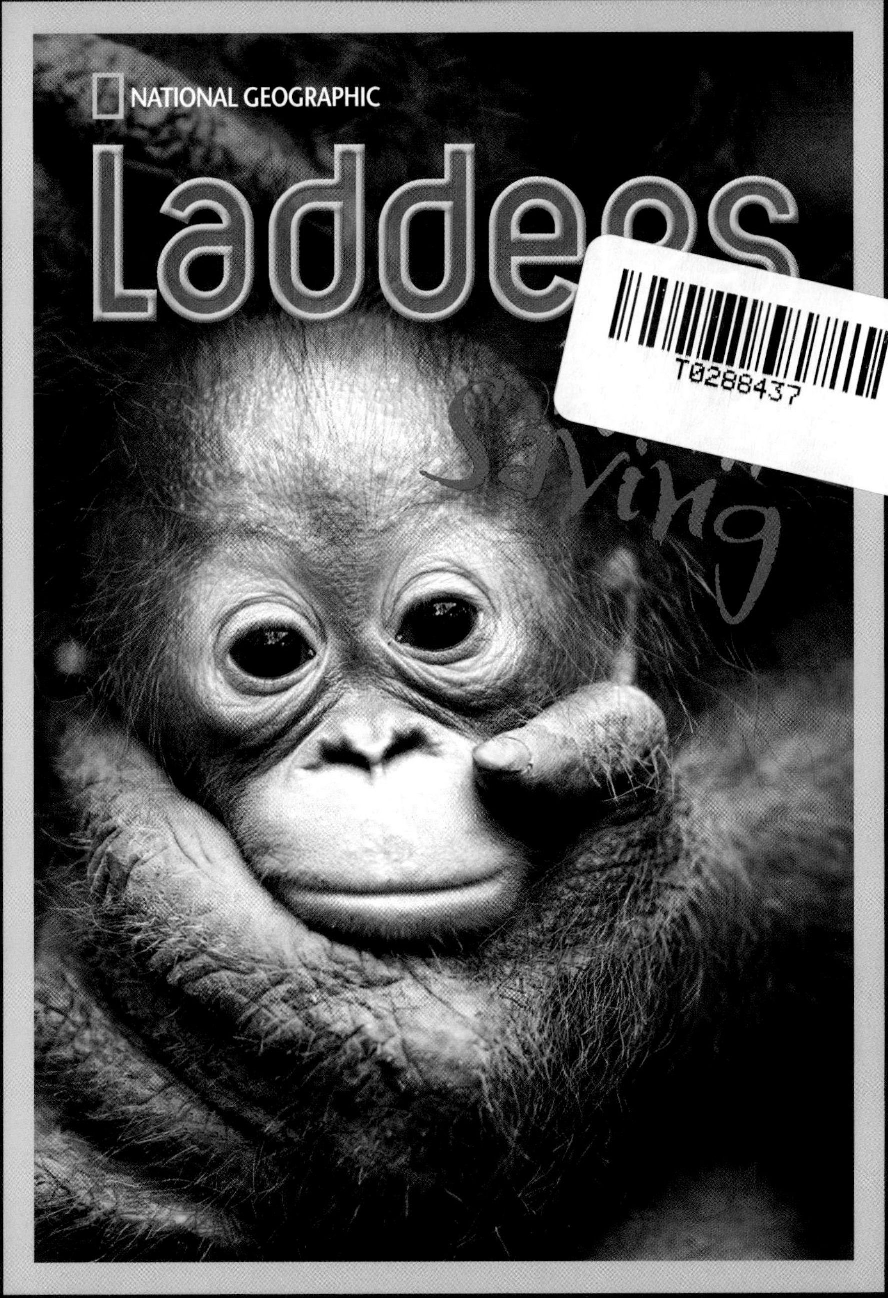
NATIONAL GEOGRAPHIC
Ladders
Saving

GENRE Science Article **Read to find out** what problems some species face.

EVERY LIVING THING

by Shirleyann Costigan

Living things are cool. They're just full of surprises! Watch the bark spider spin a gigantic web across a river. Its silk is stronger than the material used to make bulletproof vests. Take a look at the rosy periwinkle. This modest flower is used to make drugs that treat illnesses such as childhood leukemia. Check out the gribble, a tiny wood-eating worm with a big secret. The gribble produces an enzyme that may be used to develop a non-polluting fuel.

Bark spider

Rosy periwinkle

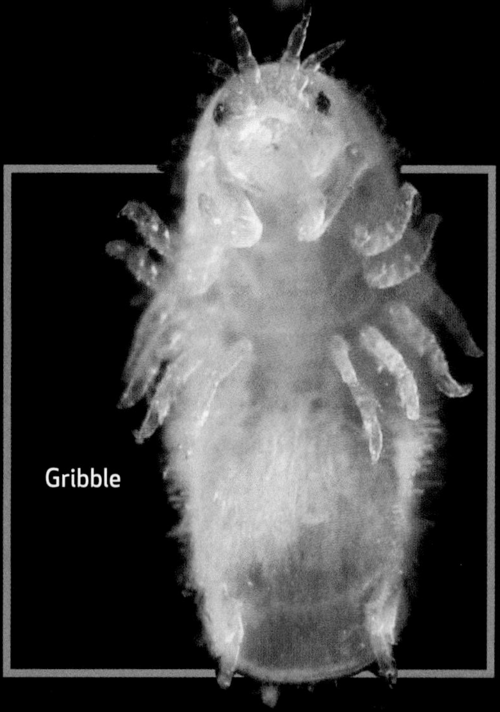

Gribble

The bark spider, rosy periwinkle, and gribble have "secrets" that could benefit humans. Luckily, these **species** are not threatened with **extinction.** Extinction is the complete loss of a species, which happens when the last living member of a species dies. Other species are **endangered,** or at risk of becoming extinct. Extinction is nothing new. Over time, as many as 99 percent of all species that ever lived on Earth have become extinct, but recently the rate has been increasing.

Extinct species are not cool. If a species becomes extinct, we will never be able to discover the benefits it may have. But what if an endangered species has no apparent benefits to humans. Does that mean it is not worth protecting?

How Endangered Is It?

EXTINCT
last member of the species has died

EXTINCT IN THE WILD
survives only in captivity

CRITICALLY ENDANGERED
extremely high risk of extinction

ENDANGERED
very high risk of extinction

VULNERABLE
high risk of extinction

NEAR THREATENED
moving toward high risk of extinction

LEAST CONCERN
no immediate threat to survival

The terms on the left are from the "Red List of Threatened Species," provided by the International Union for the **Conservation** of Nature. The list helps conservationists plan ways to save species that are at risk.

So why are so many species at risk? The biggest threat to species is the loss of natural **habitats,** and most habitat loss is caused by human activity. When people clear land for buildings or agriculture, they may destroy habitats species depend on for survival. Pollution and climate change cause habitat loss, too. Although there is no single solution, becoming aware of the problem is a starting point. The following pages reveal threats that endanger many species.

Aye-Aye Lemur

The aye-aye is a primate. *Primate* is the name of a scientific classification that also includes apes. Growing cities on the Island of Madagascar threaten the aye-aye's habitat. What's more, some people believe the aye-aye is a sign of bad luck, so they kill it on sight.

Asian Tapir

The Asian tapir may remind you of a pig with a trunk. It uses its long snout to grasp leaves in the rain forests of Southeast Asia. Habitat loss is the main cause of its dwindling population, which has decreased by over 50 percent since about 1970.

ENDANGERED

Parts of Southeast Asia

NEAR THREATENED

Parts of Madagascar

VULNERABLE

Border of Mexico and the U.S.

Star Cactus

People like this pretty little cactus, and that's one reason it's at risk. Collectors take it from the wild and sell it as a houseplant. Conservationists and others are working to protect the star cactus by growing it to sell, rather than collecting it from the wild.

Wyoming Toad

This amphibian was thought to be extinct. Then a group was discovered and used to start a captive breeding program to increase the species' population. Toads from the program are released into the wild regularly, but they face challenges, including a disease that kills amphibians.

EXTINCT IN THE WILD

Wyoming, U.S.

CRITICALLY ENDANGERED

Southeastern U.S.

Green Pitcher Plant

The tube-shaped leaves of this rare plant have liquid at the bottom. When insects fall into the liquid, they are trapped and digested. Because the plant gets nutrients from insects, it can survive in soil that has few nutrients. But will it survive threats to its land for use by agriculture, housing, and recreation?

Sapphire-bellied Hummingbird

The sapphire-bellied hummingbird is like a jewel in the tropical forests of Colombia. Unfortunately, this hummingbird is threatened by toxic pesticides and by habitat loss due to construction and the clearing of forests. Predators, such as hawks and other large birds, have reduced this species' population as well.

CRITICALLY ENDANGERED

The coast of Colombia

Giant Weta

VULNERABLE
New Zealand

The Maori people of New Zealand call it *wetapunga*, "the god of ugly things." Wetas have lived on Earth since before the dinosaurs. Although this species has survived for millions of years, its future is uncertain. Habitat loss and alien predators, such as ship rats, may finally cause its extinction.

Harlequin Mantella Frog

It looks like a Halloween decoration, so perhaps that's why this highly toxic frog is a popular pet. Hunters for the pet trade capture hundreds of harlequin mantella frogs each year. Logging and other industries have destroyed most of its natural habitat as well, and today only a few members of this colorful species still exist.

CRITICALLY ENDANGERED
Parts of Madagascar

Columbia Pygmy Rabbit

The Columbia pygmy rabbit was the smallest known rabbit in North America, and was so tiny that it could fit in your hand. A dam on the Columbia River in the state of Washington altered this species' habitat and the pygmy rabbit couldn't adapt. In 2010, the last member of this species, whose name was Bryn, died in captivity.

Saola

The Vietnamese call this beautiful ox the Asian unicorn. By the time scientists outside of Asia first learned about this species in 1992, it was already endangered. Hunters were killing it for its meat. The Vietnamese have made plans to protect the saola, but hunters are still a threat, and today only 300 or fewer saolas still exist.

Oregon Chub Minnow

The Oregon chub minnow was on the brink of extinction until the Oregon Fish and Wildlife Service came to its rescue. The Service relocated these minnows from threatened habitats to safer waters, and today the little fish are thriving!

Mekong Giant Catfish

If you ever caught a ten-foot, 400-pound freshwater fish it was probably a Mekong giant catfish. This huge fish swims in the Laos and Cambodia Mekong River Delta and is a favorite food in this part of the world. Overfishing is one reason it's critically endangered, but habitat loss caused by the building of dams and other human activity is an additional reason.

Joel Sartore

The Oregon chub minnow's success story proves one thing: we can save some of Earth's endangered species. Today many agencies are dedicated to this service. Individuals are helping too, including a photographer named Joel Sartore.

Joel Sartore photographs animals, especially animals that are endangered, for the National Geographic Society. For 20 years he has traveled around the world to record the plight of many species. His books and articles remind us that no creature is too small, too ugly, or too insignificant to matter.

Baby caiman

Check In What do you think makes a species worth saving?

GENRE Realistic Fiction

Read to find out what problem the children in this story face.

Saving Pulduny Pond

by Evelyn Stone illustrated by Nicholas Jackson

If I could speak fish, I'd grab an Oregon chub minnow and say, "Thank you, little fish for making me a hero." Sounds silly, but that's what I'd do.

My name is Kenny and I live in Puldunny, a small town in the Willamette Valley of Oregon. You won't find Puldunny on a map, but it has a school, a town hall, a main street, and a pond.

Every year, the Youth Center sponsors a community project for kids who are looking for something to do during summer vacation, or for parents who are looking for something to keep their kids busy. This year's theme was "Let's **Preserve** Puldunny," and eleven kids volunteered.

The day before the project started, I went to the pond with my friend Felicia. I call her Flea, but she doesn't really mind. Sometimes I'm slow, but Flea doesn't really mind that either because she says I have good ideas. Flea and I went to the pond to collect creepy-crawlies for her terrarium, and the mosquitoes saw us coming. Hundreds of them dive-bombed us, so we scooped up a few bugs and got outta' there.

The next day we were covered in red welts. "Mosquito bites," Flea explained to the project team, "from the pond."

"Mosquitoes can carry disease," Jamie Ealing said. "I'd never go near that scummy old pond."

"Next year you might not be able to," said Amy Franc. "My dad is on the town council, and he said they've been talking about draining the pond and are going to vote on it."

"Yes-s-s-s!" Budgie Ricks yelled. "Maybe they'll put in a skateboard park!"

"Okay, kids," interrupted Ms. Garcia. "Let's plan our project. Remember, it must preserve some part of the community, and it can't cost money. Any ideas?"

A few kids had ideas, but none of them sparked. Then Jamie said, "If we could get rid of the mosquitoes, maybe we could save Puldunny Pond."

"Fat chance," said Budgie with a sneer.

"Put a sock in it, Budge," said Flea. "It's a good idea."

"Yes it is," agreed Ms. Garcia. "Puldunny Pond is a rich **habitat** for wildlife, but Budgie's right. It would be impossible to eliminate the mosquitoes."

That's when I said, "What about the Oregon chub?"

Eleven pairs of eyes turned on me without a blink, as if aliens had zapped everyone with a stun ray.

"Yes, Kenny, go on," said Ms. Garcia.

"Well, I read that a **species** of fish called the Oregon chub minnow was **endangered** until the Fish and Wildlife Service relocated it to new habitats." My words came out slowly but no one seemed to mind so I continued.

"Maybe we could get some minnows for Puldunny Pond. The minnows would eat the mosquito larvae, and the minnows wouldn't cost any money because the relocation is free."

"That's a great idea, Ken," said Flea. "Because . . ."

"Because Kenny's your boyfriend," Budgie said with a mean grin.

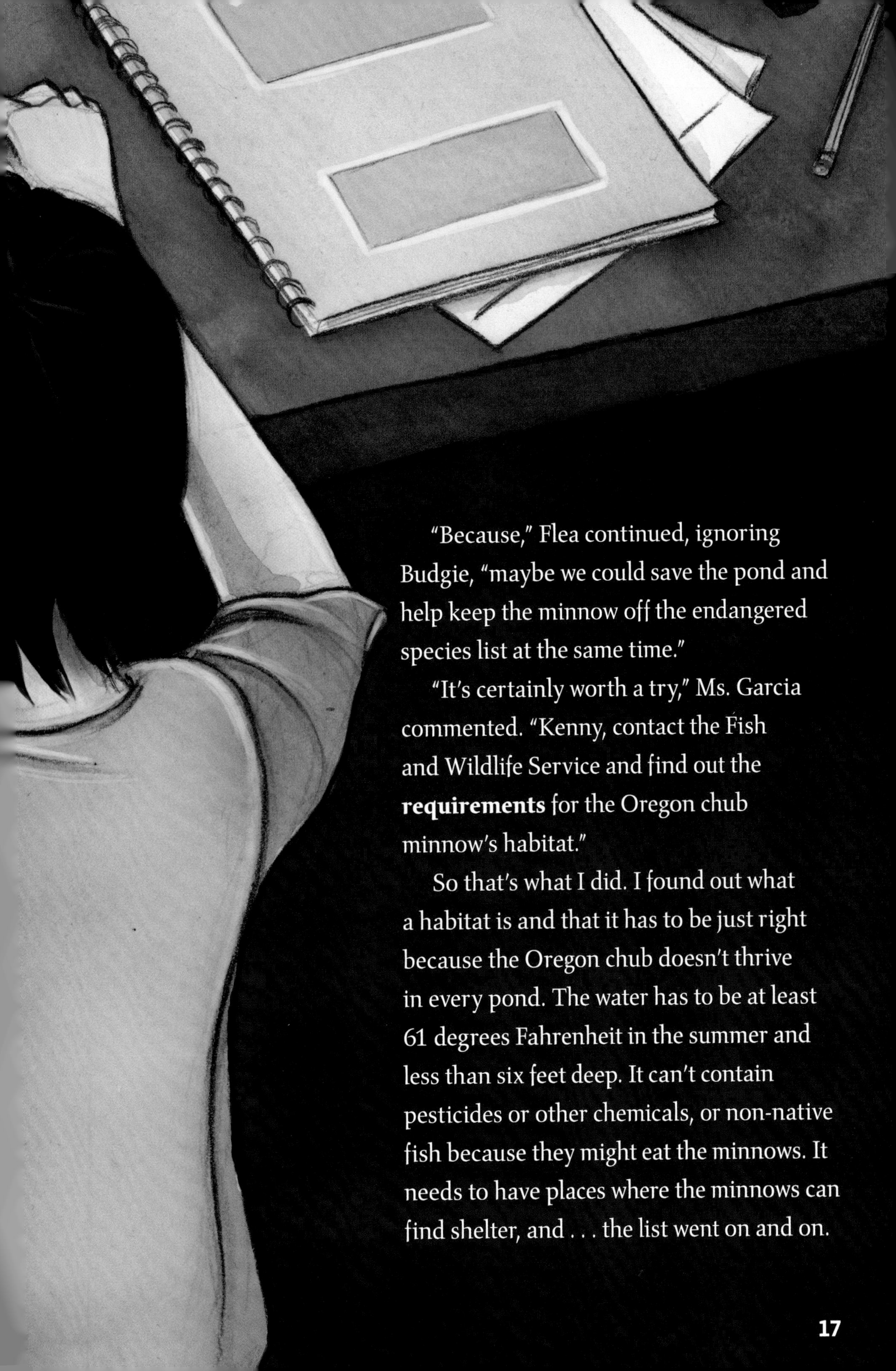

"Because," Flea continued, ignoring Budgie, "maybe we could save the pond and help keep the minnow off the endangered species list at the same time."

"It's certainly worth a try," Ms. Garcia commented. "Kenny, contact the Fish and Wildlife Service and find out the **requirements** for the Oregon chub minnow's habitat."

So that's what I did. I found out what a habitat is and that it has to be just right because the Oregon chub doesn't thrive in every pond. The water has to be at least 61 degrees Fahrenheit in the summer and less than six feet deep. It can't contain pesticides or other chemicals, or non-native fish because they might eat the minnows. It needs to have places where the minnows can find shelter, and . . . the list went on and on.

"We can't do it," I told the team the next day. "There are too many requirements, so I don't think Puldunny Pond is the right habitat." I thought I sounded very scientific.

"We don't know we can't," said Flea. "Let's take a closer look at the pond and find out."

"Why bother," said Budgie. "It won't work."

"Maybe it won't," Ms. Garcia replied. "But at least we will have tried."

So the next day, covered in protective clothing and loads of insect repellent, we all marched to the pond. Amy Franc's dad let us use his rowboat and came along to make sure no one fell overboard.

The team measured the depth and temperature of the pond, collected silt and water samples, and made a record of the plants, fish, and insects living in and around the pond. And that's not all. Back at the Youth Center, we wrote a report that included lists and graphs and all kinds of scientific stuff, like the names of the species we found. It took days! Budgie snuck out a few times, but Ms. Garcia said he'd be an endangered species if he did it again. Finally we finished our report and sent to the Fish and Wildlife Service.

A week later, two agents from the Fish and Wildlife Service went to the pond, collected more samples, and then stopped by the Youth Center to ask a few questions. They left us biting our nails, and even Budgie worried that we would fail.

A few weeks passed without a word, but Ms. Garcia finally received an email saying that the Oregon Fish and Wildlife Service would relocate five hundred Oregon chubs from the Dexter Reservoir to Puldunny Pond. We'd done it!

Amy Franc's dad stopped by with more good news. "The town council decided to postpone the vote on draining the pond," he announced. "We're going to wait until next summer." He paused and watched as I scratched a mosquito bite I got when we were in his rowboat collecting water samples. Then he teased, "We'll send you to the pond, Kenny. If you return without any mosquito bites, then we'll know that your plan succeeded!"

We all went to the pond to watch when the agents released the tiny fish. Flea said I was a hero because the minnow idea was mine, and she just knew the minnows were going to save the pond. She even gave me a new name. She calls me Chub.

Now if only I could speak fish.

Check In How did Kenny and the other children solve their problem?

GENRE Fantasy

Read to find out what problems the STARS face.

STARS
Wild and Free

by Grace O'Brien
illustrated by Matt Luxich

In a secluded location in the wilderness, a group of animals gathered. Most had never ventured beyond their own **habitats** before, but an urgent mission brought them together from all parts of the globe.

"We're here because our **species** are at risk," said HB, the helmeted hornbill, from the podium. "Humans have labeled us '**endangered**' or 'threatened,' yet they aren't coming to our rescue. Instead, they help the **celebrity** animals. You know the types—furry animals, like pandas; beautiful animals, like penguins; and majestic animals like hawks. We're going to change that!"

The cheering animals didn't fit the description of celebrities. They weren't furry, beautiful, or majestic. In fact, they were a variety pack of oddballs. Some had spines instead of fur, some had unusual features, and some just seemed too small to matter.

HB continued, "We may not be celebrities, but we are STARS—Super Terrific At-Risk Species." Then he challenged the crowd, "Who are we?"

"STARS!" they shouted.

STARS
SUPER TERRIFIC AT-RISK SPECIES
ENDANGERED AND SICK OF IT!
SNACK

“We’re going to hear from several STARS today,” HB said, and introduced the speakers. The audience listened as a duck-billed platypus, an aye-aye lemur, and a tapir told about threats to their species. As they spoke, a map on a video screen glowed with red dots that showed the locations of their threatened habitats.

“And now, one final speaker!” said HB, and all eyes were drawn to the Mekong giant catfish who appeared on the screen before them. The huge catfish was almost one hundred years old, but a neighboring school of fish had taught him how to video chat.

Bubble, bubble. In a deep, murky voice he began slowly, “Don’t give up! Humans can help. Tell them your stories,” he gurgled through the cloudy water of a river far away. “And then,” he added, “tell the stories over and over again around the world.”

The connection was lost and the screen faded to black, but the ancient giant's words inspired the audience. They had to think of a plan that would help them all avoid extinction . . . *fast!*

"He's right," said Edna, the echidna, in a thin voice. "We need to tell our stories to humans. Why don't we do what Mr. Mekong did and use a camera to tell about our unusual but amazing selves?" Then Edna got louder, as if she really started to believe in her idea.

And so it was decided. The STARS formed a film crew and set out to make a documentary about how their habitats and lives were threatened. The crew filmed in forests and fields, deserts and jungles, mountains and valleys.

A year later, the documentary was ready, and none too soon since more STARS were at risk and habitats were shrinking.

"Now how can we get humans to watch our documentary?" wondered HB as he paced back and forth in their makeshift studio in the wilderness. As he paced, a pair of binoculars fell from a branch overhead.

"What's this?" he cried, then looked up to discover a human high up in the tree. The human had learned of the animals' secluded location and was snooping around in hope of sighting the at-risk species.

"Oh my!" exclaimed the human, and she quickly climbed down.

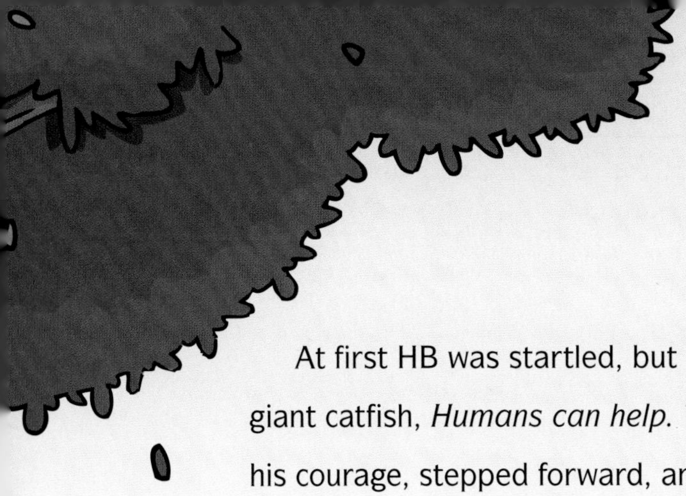

At first HB was startled, but then he recalled the words of the giant catfish, *Humans can help. Tell them your stories.* He summoned his courage, stepped forward, and told his story, beginning with memories of the habitat he knew when he was a hatchling, describing changes since then, and telling about the STARS' mission. The other animals gathered around and followed his example.

The woman was moved. "I'm a scientist," she explained. "My mission is to help endangered species, and I'd like to help you."

The animals were excited, and soon they were chattering with the scientist like old friends. Next, a meeting was arranged to show the documentary to humans in a city far away.

A few weeks passed and the first-time filmmakers arrived in the city. They were nervous as they walked through the unfamiliar habitat with buildings and cars everywhere, but they trusted the scientist and followed her up a flight of stairs into a building with a sign that said "National Geographic Society."

HB felt at ease when he met the scientist's friends, humans who were curious about the at-risk species and eager to see their documentary. The human in charge led them to a room with theater-style seats, a big screen, and posters of documentaries starring penguins, lions, and other celebrity animals dotting the walls.

"These humans have made a lot of movies," HB thought, "but I don't see any with STARS! If they could help get our documentary into theaters, our species might have a chance."

Edna set up the film and the lights went out. An hour later, the screen went dark and the lights came back on. After a tense pause, the human in charge turned to HB and said, "This film has action, excitement, and exotic animals. I love it! What should we call it?"

"How about *STARS Wild and Free*?" HB responded.

"You've got it!" the human exclaimed.

It didn't take long until movie posters were hanging in theaters across the nation. Humans and animals of all kinds lined up to see it, and soon humans far and wide were finding ways to protect these amazing animals.

Check In How did the STARS solve their problem?

Discuss Cause and Effect and Point of View

1. According to "Every Living Thing," what is the main cause of habitat loss?

2. Choose one species in "Every Living Thing." What is the effect of habitat loss on this species?

3. Identify the point of view from which "Saving Puldunny Pond" and "STARS Wild and Free" are told. Which is first-person? Which is third-person? Compare and contrast the point of view.

4. If you had to choose one species to protect, which species would it be? Why?